£5.99
UK Only

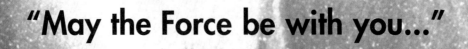

"May the Force be with you..."

STAR WARS ANNUAL 1998 OWNERSHIP DATA

This book belongs to..

Age...

Address...

....

Planet...

Copyright © Lucasfilm Ltd 1997
Licensed by Lucasfilm Ltd
All rights reserved.

Published in Great Britain in 1997 by
World International Ltd., Deanway Technology Centre,
Wilmslow Road, Handforth, Cheshire SK9 3FB.
Printed in Great Britain. ISBN 0 7498 3395 5

Designed by Simon Connor
Compiled by John Broadhead and Joyce McAleer

DARTH VADER

LUKE SKYWALKER

OBI-WAN KENOBI

HAN SOLO

CHEWBACCA

CONTENTS

PRINCESS LEIA

LANDO CALRISSIAN

C-3PO

STORMTROOPER

YODA

R2-D2

BOBA FETT

Long ago in a galaxy far, far away....
Important events in the history of Star Wars

25,000 years BSW4
(Before *Star Wars IV: A New Hope*)
Beginning of the Old Republic and a period of peace in the galaxy. Jedi Knights first appear.

896 BSW4
Birth of Yoda,
Jedi Master.

55 BSW4
Birth of Anakin Skywalker,
father of Luke and Leia.

200 BSW4
Birth of Chewbacca the
Wookiee on Kashyyyk.

60 BSW4
Birth of Obi-Wan Kenobi,
Jedi Knight.

48 BSW4
Birth of Mon Mothma,
leader of the Rebel Alliance

29 BSW4
Birth of Han Solo in the
Corellian star system. Fall
of the Republic
A dark period when
corruption and injustice
sweep through the
Republic. Senator Palpatine
rises to power.

18 BSW4
Birth of Luke Skywalker and Leia
Organa, who are put into hiding.
Anakin Skywalker becomes Darth
Vader; The Empire is formed, with
Palpatine as Emperor. The first
stirrings of rebellion begin.

3 ASW4
(*Star Wars V: The
Empire Strikes Back*)
Battle of Hoth. Luke
confronts Darth Vader.
Han Solo is captured by
Boba Fett.

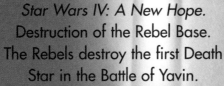

Star Wars IV: A New Hope.
Destruction of the Rebel Base.
The Rebels destroy the first Death
Star in the Battle of Yavin.

35 BSW4
End of the Clone Wars,
a violent conflict in which
the Jedi Knights fight to
defend the Old Republic.
Obi-Wan Kenobi and
Anakin Skywalker emerge
as heroes.

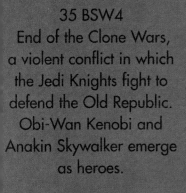

4 ASW4
The events of *Star Wars VI: Return of the Jedi.*
Han Solo is freed and Jabba the Hutt dies.
The Emperor dies, too, when Darth Vader turns
against him. The Battle of Endor and the
destruction of the Death Star ends the Galactic
Civil War. The New Republic is formed.

REBEL PROFILE

Name: Leia Organa
Genus: Human
Hair: Brown
Eyes: Brown
Height: 1.52 metres
Home: Alderaan

The brave and beautiful Princess Leia is a cell-leader in the Rebel Alliance, and a driving force in its continuing struggle against the evil Empire.

When her father, the star pilot Anakin Skywalker, turned to the dark side of the Force, baby Leia and her twin brother Luke were hidden for safety. Leia was brought by Obi-Wan Kenobi to Alderaan, where she was adopted by Bail Organa and grew up as a princess in the Royal House.

She rises quickly to become a Senator for the Old Republic, but her strong sense of justice persuades her to work secretly with Mon Mothma, her colleague, to help create the Rebel Alliance.

It is on a Rebel mission that we first meet her in *Star Wars IV: A New Hope*. She is on the way to Tatooine to find Obi-Wan Kenobi and ask him to join the cause...

Leia in a scene from
The Empire Strikes Back

Leia and Chewbacca
at the controls of the
Millennium Falcon

PRINCESS LEIA

REBEL PROFILE

Name: Luke Skywalker
Genus: Human
Hair: Blonde
Eyes: Blue
Height: 1.72 metres
Home: Tatooine

Luke Skywalker is the valiant young farm boy who destroys the terrible Death Star!

He was taken to Tatooine as a baby and brought up by Owen and Beru Lars, whom he understood to be his uncle and aunt. But a quiet life on the farm is not for him - he longs to be a pilot, and his dream is to join the Imperial Space Academy.

Fate lends a hand when Luke's uncle buys R2-D2 and C-3PO from Jawa traders. Luke is captivated by Leia's plea for help in a holographic image from R2-D2 - he doesn't yet know, of course, that she's his sister - and he sets off on the adventure of a lifetime to save her.

He goes on to become a celebrated Rebel hero, commanding a crack X-wing squadron and learns the secrets of the Force when he takes instruction from Yoda, the old Jedi Master.

Luke after landing on Dagobah

Luke in his trusty landspeeder

LUKE SKYWALKER

REBEL PROFILE

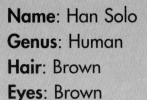

Name: Han Solo
Genus: Human
Hair: Brown
Eyes: Brown
Height: 1.83 metres
Home: Corellia

He's an ace space pilot, smuggler, adventurer and gambler. Han Solo can turn his skilful hand to virtually anything, as long as it carries a strong element of risk and danger - and the price is right. Even his battered freighter, the *Millennium Falcon*, was won from his friend Lando in a game!

Dry-humoured Han may appear arrogant and hard, but he certainly has a soft centre. When he agrees to speed Luke and Obi-Wan Kenobi to Alderaan, he becomes embroiled in the rescue of Leia from the clutches of Darth Vader.

He falls hopelessly in love with Leia and fights by her side for the Alliance. It's a long, hard struggle, and at one point Han is carbon-frozen and kept as a wall-hanging trophy by the repulsive gangster Jabba the Hutt.

But, thanks to his Rebel companions, it's yet another scrape he manages to get out of. He returns to duty and plays a vital role in the crucial Battle of Endor, which restores freedom to the galaxy.

Han frozen in carbonite ready for his trip to Jabba's palace

HAN SOLO

REBEL PROFILE

Name: Obi-Wan Kenobi
Genus: Human
Hair: Grey
Eyes: Brown
Height: 1.75 metres
Home: Tatooine

The mysterious, robed hermit Ben is in reality the wise Obi-Wan Kenobi, Jedi Knight and a distinguished general in the Clone Wars.

After his good friend Anakin Skywalker was lured to the Emperor's side, Ben remained living close to young Luke on Tatooine, sensing that the child was to be the last hope for the galaxy.

His instinct proves right, for Luke comes searching for him in an effort to free Princess Leia from the Death Star.

Ben is Luke's first tutor in the secrets of the Force, a natural field of energy which permeates the whole of the galaxy and binds it together. The Force may be used in various ways: for knowledge, seeing afar, sensing danger and even levitation. The light side of the Force was used by the Jedi Knights for peace and harmony; but its dark side can be exploited for aggression, as Ben's powerful adversary Darth Vader demonstrates so clearly.

Ben showing Luke the weapon of a Jedi

OBI-WAN KENOBI

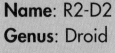

REBEL PROFILE

Name: R2-D2
Genus: Droid
Hair: Not Applicable
Eye Sensor: Red
Height: 0.96 metres
Home: Not known

Beep, whirr, whistle! This friendly little brainbox with a quirky personality all his own is an astromech droid. And although he relies on C-3PO to translate his speech, he fully understands everything going on around him.

His head dome rotates a full 360 degrees and houses a hologram projector; and his body is packed with sophisticated sensors and invaluable gadgets. Note his third leg, which springs into action to keep him upright when the going gets tough!

Name: C-3PO
Genus: Droid
Hair: Not Applicable
Eye sensors: Yellow
Height: 1.68 metres
Home: Not known

At first glance C-3PO looks like a knight in shining armour. But this impeccably mannered golden boy is more likely to be found fussing over R2-D2's wayward behaviour than planning a battle!

He's a polite fellow by design: a protocol droid, specially programmed to interact with humans, conversing and translating in his bright, chirpy voice. And he's certainly good at his job - he can speak more than six million galactic languages!

R2-D2 / C-3PO

REBEL PROFILE

Name: Chewbacca
Genus: Wookiee
Hair: Brown
Eyes: Blue
Height: 2.29 metres
Home: Kashyyyk

What do you say to a huge and immensely strong creature covered in thick, shaggy hair? How about "please" and "thank you", for a start!

Despite the awesome growls and grunts, 200-year-old Chewbacca is the devoted buddy of Han, who saved him from a life of slavery. Chewie is handy with his fists and his bowcaster weapon, and he's a skilled pilot and brilliant mechanic too. What more could you really ask for in a friend...?

Name: Jawas
Genus: Jawa
Hair: Not known
Eyes: Yellow
Height: 0.96 metres average
Home: Tatooine

The jabbering little Jawas are harmless enough to you and me, though R2-D2 and C-3PO would hardly agree. For Jawas are travelling merchants who make their living by scavenging for hardware - including droids - which they repair and then sell.

Actually it's a lucky break when the Jawas capture R2-D2 and C-3PO and sell them to Luke. Otherwise, the future of the galaxy would be very different indeed...

CHEWBACCA / JAWA

GALAXY PROFILE

Name: Jabba the Hutt
Genus: Hutt
Hair: None
Eyes: Orange
Height: 1.75 metres
Home: Nal Hutta

Jabba, a huge, slug of a gangster, is the slimiest crime lord you could imagine - and the least likely to make a quick getaway!

He operates in considerable comfort on Tatooine, from his large palace filled with servants and ghastly criminal cronies from all over the galaxy. Beneath his throne room is a pit in which he keeps his pet rancor, a huge and terrifying reptilian monster which feeds on anyone who displeases Jabba...

Name: Tusken Raiders
Genus: Humanoid
Hair: Not known
Eyes: Not known
Height: 1.9 metres average
Home: Tatooine

Tusken Raiders, also known as Sand People, are terrors of the Tatooine desert. They are covered from top to toe in a headwrap, ragged cloak and a special breathing mask which also provides protection for their eyes. Quite what they look like underneath, no one is quite sure!

Skilled in survival and carrying gaderffii stick weapons, they lead a nomadic existence wandering the Tatooine wastes in groups. They travel on banthas - huge four-legged beasts covered in long, rough fur.

JABBA THE HUTT/TUSKEN RAIDER

EMPIRE PROFILE

Name: Darth Vader
Genus: Human
Hair: None
Eyes: Not known
Height: 2.03 metres
Home: Not known

The mighty Darth Vader, Dark Lord of the Sith, is an awe-inspiring figure, feared not only by the Rebels but by his own subordinates too.

Once the best starfighter plot in the galaxy, Anakin Skywalker, he was trained in the Jedi arts by his friend Obi-Wan Kenobi. But he became greedy for power and absconded to the dark side.

Obi-Wan Kenobi tried in vain to win him back. The two fought, and Anakin fell into a molten pit, to emerge a scarred and broken man. Unable to breathe unaided, he designed a life-supporting helmet and adopted body armour and sweeping black cloak. Darth Vader was born!

Lord Vader was assigned to kill the remaining Jedi Knights and assisted in the construction of the Death Star. Now, as commander of the Imperial Fleet, his mission is deadly simple: to hunt down the Rebel leaders and destroy them. Unfortunately for Darth Vader, the most prominent members of the Alliance are his son Luke and daughter Leia.

DARTH VADER

EMPIRE PROFILE

Name: Grand Moff Tarkin
Genus: Human
Hair: Black
Eyes: Brown
Height: 1.83 metres
Home: Not known

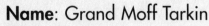

Just a glance into the eyes of the grim and gaunt-faced Governor Tarkin will tell you that he rules by fear! This cold and ruthless man is totally committed to the Emperor.

He conceived the idea for the Death Star and saw it through to completion. Heartless Tarkin has no misgivings when it comes to ordering the termination of Princess Leia... nor when destroying her home planet simply as a display of power.

Name: Stormtroopers
Genus: Human
Hair: Various
Eyes: Various
Height: 1.83 metres average
Home: Various

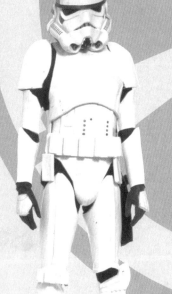

The distinctive white armour of Imperial stormtroopers hides the darkest of hearts. You can't reason with these unyielding shock troops. They're selected for their unquestioning loyalty to the Empire and are willing to run straight into the firing-line without fear for their lives. They wear a special temperature-controlled body glove under an 18-piece spacesuit, which permits them to perform their heinous duties in virtually any conditions.

GRAND MOFF TARKIN / STORMTROOPER

THE STAR WARS SAGA CONTINUES!

When *Star Wars* first hit cinema screens back in 1977 it was nothing short of a sensation. It won six Academy Awards, becoming the highest grossing film of the time. *The Empire Strikes Back* followed, and then *Return of the Jedi* broke yet another record at the box-office.

This phenomenal space trilogy was the brainchild of the talented and imaginative George Lucas, the single-minded director who had an ambitious

vision of a fantastic and mind-blowing cinematic experience. He knew precisely what his public wanted: fantastic adventure, excitement, spectacular visual and sound effects plus handsome heroes and even a beautiful princess! Young George wanted to be an illustrator - until he discovered the magic of making movies, that is. At film-school he rapidly became a star in his own right, going on after graduation to write and direct the highly acclaimed *American Graffiti*.

His *Star Wars* films became a world-wide hit, with numerous spin-off novels, comic books and a wide range of avidly-collected toys and models. But a whole new generation of fans had grown up without ever seeing the movies on the big screen.
And so, in 1995, George Lucas began a labour of love - the production of the new, digitally remastered Special Editions.
High-tech computer technology had arrived, and this gave George Lucas the perfect opportunity to remake the films exactly as he had envisaged them.

The original negatives were cleaned and restored, and then his innovative special effects company Industrial Light & Magic began the painstaking work of combining computer-generated visuals with existing footage. The effects we had seen some twenty years before, using models flown by wires, had thrilled

audiences. But now, enhanced by computer wizardry, they would be awe-inspiring. And they are! In the Special Edition of *Star Wars: A New Hope*, Mos Eisley has been transformed into a much busier, thriving spaceport bristling with life - in a rich variety of forms. In *Return of the Jedi*, the musical interlude in Jabba's palace has been enlivened and extended, and brand-new characters have been generated to interact with the band. Originally Jabba the Hutt didn't make his appearance until the third film, but now we meet him in *Star Wars: A New Hope*. George Lucas had filmed a sequence where Han

encountered Jabba at Mos Eisley. A stand-in actor played the part of Jabba, subsequently destined to be replaced by an animated version of the sluglike crime lord. Unfortunately time and budget constraints made the scene impossible- until now. In the Special Edition, Han acts and chats, guardedly, with his adversary, even

walking round the back of him and stepping on his tail!

George Lucas has not directed a movie for twenty years, but now he is hard at work on the new *Star Wars* movies. From his home base at Skywalker Ranch, in California, he is masterminding the filming of the next three movies. These are 'prequels' which will relate the early years of Luke's father Anakin: how he met Ben and became a Jedi Knight before turning to the dark side and then adopting the fearsome persona of Darth Vader.

The *Star Wars* galaxy may be far, far away but it's a place we just can't wait to visit again as soon as possible. And one thing's for sure: with George Lucas at the controls, we're in for some unforgettable trips skyward!

STAR WARS
A NEW HOPE

It is a period of civil war. Rebel spaceships, striking from a hidden base, have won their first victory against the evil Galactic Empire.

During the battle, Rebel spies manage to steal secret plans to the Empire's ultimate weapon, the Death Star, an armoured space station with enough power to destroy an entire planet.

Pursued by the Empire's sinister agents, Princess Leia

races home aboard her starship, custodian of the stolen plans that could save her people and restore freedom to the galaxy...

Darth Vader closed in fast on the Rebel starship.

Princess Leia hastily put the vital Death Star plans into R2-D2's memory. As the Imperial troopers blasted

their way into the ship, R2-D2 rolled into an escape pod, followed by C-3PO.

The pod landed in a desert region of Tatooine. Artoo trundled off into the high land. "I'm not going that way!" announced

Threepio, heading in another direction. But they were soon together again, captured by the Jawas and sold off to Luke Skywalker and his farmer uncle.

As Luke cleaned up Artoo, the little droid projected a hologram of Princess Leia. "Help me, Obi-Wan Kenobi," she pleaded.

When Luke went off to eat, Artoo made his escape to search for Obi-Wan. Next morning Luke and Threepio raced off in pursuit. In the desert they were attacked by Tusken Raiders. Luke fell back, stunned. But then Ben, an old, bearded hermit, appeared and chased away the aggressors.

He was Obi-Wan Kenobi!

Luke played Leia's hologram to Ben. "This is our most desperate hour," said the Princess, explaining that the secret plans in Artoo had to be delivered to her father on the planet Alderaan in order to save the galaxy from the Empire.

Luke returned to the farm. It  was a smoking ruin, and Luke's aunt and uncle were dead. Vader's men had been searching for the two droids and the plans!

Soon Luke, Ben and the droids arrived at the pilots' bar in Mos Eisley spaceport. There they found an adventurer named Han Solo and his huge, hairy partner Chewbacca, who agreed to take them to Alderaan. Han took them all on board his  battered freighter *Millennium Falcon*. Vader's troopers arrived and rushed at them, but the *Falcon* flew away just in time.

Meanwhile, the immense Death Star battle station, now with Leia as a prisoner, flew near Alderaan. The cruel Governor Tarkin demanded that she tell him the location of the Rebel Base. If not, he would destroy Alderaan.

She answered, untruthfully, but Tarkin was heartless. "Commence primary ignition," he snapped, and a beam of energy flashed from the Death Star's superlaser and blew 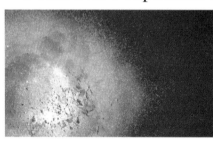 Leia's home planet to pieces.

The *Millennium Falcon* had been approaching Alderaan. Now it was pulled by a powerful tractor beam into the Death Star. When Vader strode aboard the ship, it appeared empty. "I want every part of this ship checked," he growled.

After Vader left, Luke, Ben, Han and Chewie emerged from a hatch in the floor. To escape, they would have to find the tractor beam switch. Han lured two guards on board. Luke and Han took their uniforms.

Then the Rebels and droids crept into the Death Star. Artoo plugged into  a computer socket and discovered the position of the tractor beam switch. "I must go alone," said Ben, slipping away. Artoo beeped and whistled. "He's found the Princess on the fifth level!" Threepio interpreted. Han

and Luke, now dressed as guards, took Chewie 'prisoner' and set off to find Leia.

Ben clambered up a shaft in the Death Star and switched off the tractor beam. Suddenly he felt the presence of danger...and Darth Vader

appeared with his deadly lightsabre! Ben went for him with his own lightsabre. The two fought on and on. Everyone came running to watch. Suddenly Vader struck at Ben, who smiled knowingly. The lightsabre sliced his cloak in two - but Ben was gone!

Luke, Han, Leia and the droids raced to the

Falcon, now free to fly. They made straight for the Rebel Base on the planet Yavin, with

the Death Star tracking them, as Leia suspected would happen.

At the Base, the Rebels

studied the plans and found the single weak spot in the Death Star: a vent through

which a torpedo would cause a chain reaction and destroy the main reactor. They would attack, and quickly, for the Death Star was approaching...and only fifteen minutes away.

The pilots took to the air. As Luke climbed aboard his X-wing, he

heard Ben's voice reminding him, "The Force will be with you..."

The Rebel ships rushed at the Death Star but many were blasted away by its batteries of weapons and Imperial TIE fighters. Soon only Luke remained, and he raced along a narrow canyon, on target for the vent. But Darth Vader was hot on his tail and about to deploy a crippling

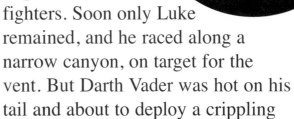

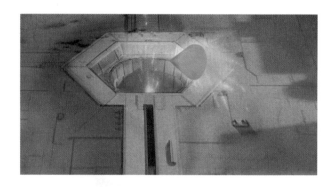

blast of laser fire.

Suddenly Vader's ship was hit - by Han in the *Falcon*! Vader spun wildly out of control and somersaulted into space. Luke was all clear! He heard Ben's voice again, telling him to forget the

computer and rely on the Force to guide him.

Inside the Death Star, things were hotting up. Governor Tarkin was about to annihilate the Rebel Base, when evacuation was suggested. "Evacuate? In our moment of triumph?" he exclaimed incredulously.

Luke launched his torpedoes. Bam! they hit the target, and he shot away at full speed.

The monumental explosion of the reactor followed...and the Death Star, together with its evil occupants, were gone!

On their return to the planet, Luke, Han and Chewbacca were the heroes of the day. Luke and Han were presented with medals by Princess Leia to show how grateful the people were.

The Planet Tatooine

There's no shortage of sunshine on Tatooine - it has two suns! This arid desert of

a planet is in the Outer Rim Territories of the galaxy. It's distant enough from the Empire's oppressive regime to make it the ideal spot for all manner of racketeers, smugglers and bounty hunters, including, of course, Jabba the Hutt.

Luke considers Tatooine to be a backwater and is aching to leave for some action, adventure and bright lights. He has grown up there with Owen and Beru Lars, who, like many of the human population, earn their living by moisture farming. This involves removing precious water from the air and then either selling it off for drinking or using it

for the irrigation of crops. In addition to the little Jawas roaming around in their huge sandcrawlers, the desert is home to the hostile Sand People, who pose a continuous threat of attack...

Mos Eisley

If you really want to see life - in a rich variety of forms - then Mos Eisley is the place to go! There's never any shortage of pilots and galactic travellers coming and going in Tatooine's only spaceport. This is a tough city of docking bays, buying and selling, and many a shady underworld deal.

One of the favourite haunts for visitors and general resident low-life in Mos Eisley is the Cantina. It's a rowdy, rough and ready kind of place, like a cowboy saloon in space. The golden rule is to steer clear of trouble and look the other way when things turn nasty.

Luke discovers this all too soon when he steps up to the bar and is picked on by a gruesome alien. Ben tries to resolve the situation peacefully but is forced to use his lightsabre to save the day.

More violence erupts shortly afterwards when Greedo, one of Jabba's murderous bounty hunters, arrives at the Cantina to kill Han Solo. Han shoots, apologising for the mess as he leaves!

The Death Star

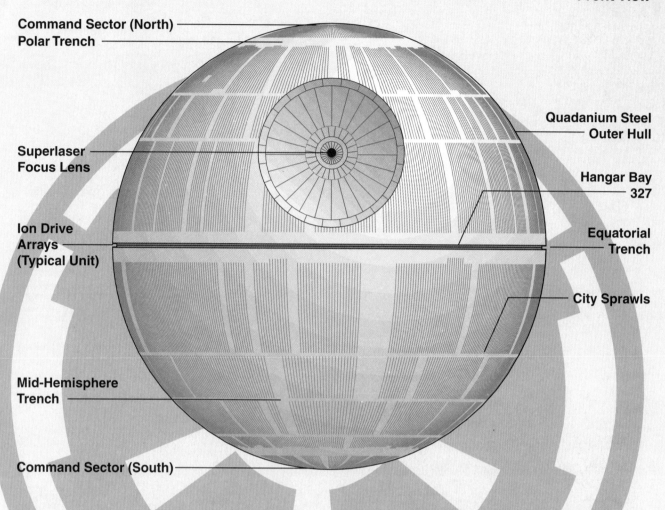

Command Sector (North)

Polar Trench

Quadanium Steel
Outer Hull

Superlaser
Focus Lens

Hangar Bay
327

Ion Drive
Arrays
(Typical Unit)

Equatorial
Trench

City Sprawls

Mid-Hemisphere
Trench

Command Sector (South)

Size: 120 kilometres diameter
Crew: 265,675 plus 57,276 gunners
Passengers: 843,342
Weapons: 1 superlaser; 5,000 turbolaser
batteries; 5,000 heavy turbo
lasers; 2,500 laser cannons;
768 tractor beam
emplacements;
2,500 ion cannons

EMPIRE PROFILE

Star Destroyer

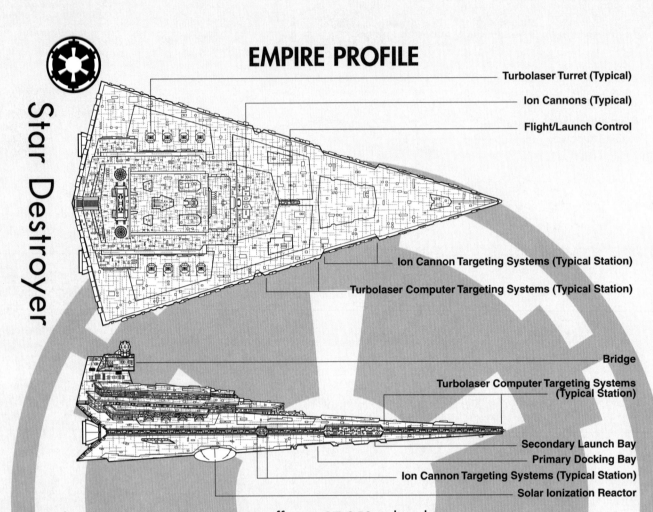

Turbolaser Turret (Typical)

Ion Cannons (Typical)

Flight/Launch Control

Ion Cannon Targeting Systems (Typical Station)

Turbolaser Computer Targeting Systems (Typical Station)

Bridge

Turbolaser Computer Targeting Systems (Typical Station)

Secondary Launch Bay

Primary Docking Bay

Ion Cannon Targeting Systems (Typical Station)

Solar Ionization Reactor

Length: 1,600 metres **Crew**: 9,235 officers, 27,850 enlisted
Passengers: 9,700 troops **Weapons**: 60 turbolaser batteries;
60 ion cannons; 10 tractor beam projectors

Length: 6.3 metres
Crew: 1 pilot
Passengers: none
Weapons: 2 laser cannons

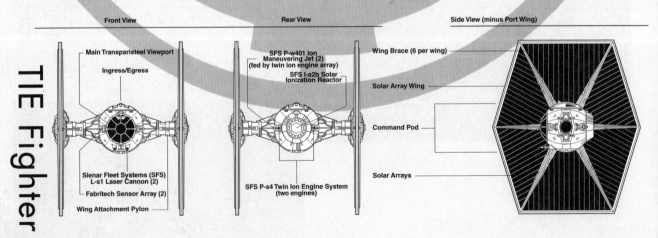

Front View

Main Transparisteel Viewport

Ingress/Egress

Sienar Fleet Systems (SFS)
L-s1 Laser Cannon (2)

Fabritech Sensor Array (2)

Wing Attachment Pylon

Rear View

SFS P-w401 Ion
Maneuvering Jet (2)
(fed by twin ion engine array)

SFS I-a2b Solar
Ionization Reactor

SFS P-s4 Twin Ion Engine System
(two engines)

Side View (minus Port Wing)

Wing Brace (6 per wing)

Solar Array Wing

Command Pod

Solar Arrays

TIE Fighter

26

REBEL PROFILE

Front View

Concussion Missile Tubes (2)

Forward Mandibles

Equipment Access Bay (4)

Deflector Shield Projector

Sensor Dish

Forward Floodlight

Quad Laser Cannon

Cockpit

Escape Pods

Armor Plating

Drive Units

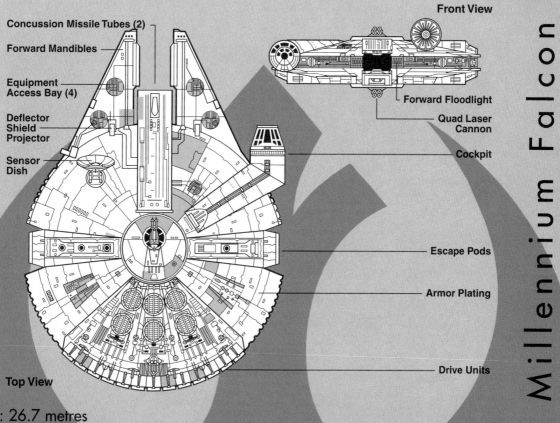

Top View

Length: 26.7 metres

Crew: 2 minimum

Passengers: 6

Weapons: 2 quad laser cannons; 2 concussion missile tubes; blaster cannon

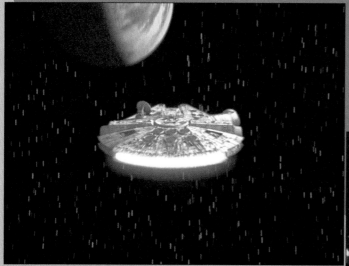

The *Millennium Falcon* approaches Yavin Four

TIE Fighters chase the *Millennium Falcon* into an asteroid field

X-wing Fighter

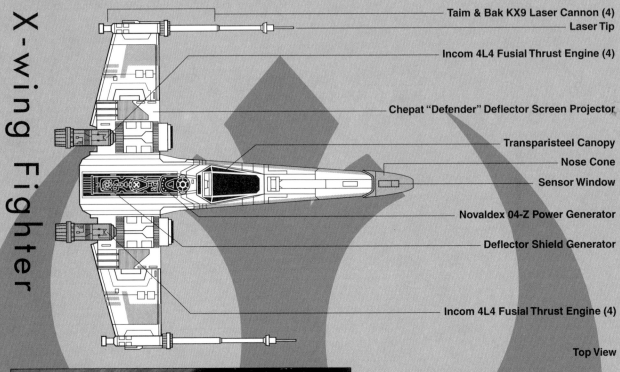

Taim & Bak KX9 Laser Cannon (4)
Laser Tip

Incom 4L4 Fusial Thrust Engine (4)

Chepat "Defender" Deflector Screen Projector

Transparisteel Canopy
Nose Cone
Sensor Window

Novaldex 04-Z Power Generator

Deflector Shield Generator

Incom 4L4 Fusial Thrust Engine (4)

Top View

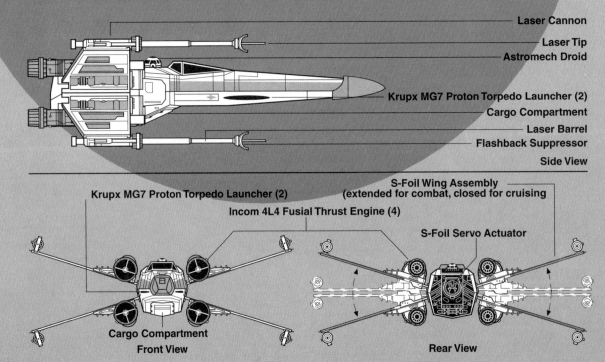

Length: 12.5 metres
Crew: 1 plus 1 astromech droid
Passengers: none
Weapons: 4 laser cannons;
2 proton torpedo launchers

Laser Cannon
Laser Tip
Astromech Droid

Krupx MG7 Proton Torpedo Launcher (2)
Cargo Compartment
Laser Barrel
Flashback Suppressor

Side View

S-Foil Wing Assembly
(extended for combat, closed for cruising

Krupx MG7 Proton Torpedo Launcher (2)

Incom 4L4 Fusial Thrust Engine (4)

S-Foil Servo Actuator

Cargo Compartment
Front View

Rear View

REBEL PROFILE

Length: 16 metres

Crew: 2 plus 1 astromech droid

Passengers: none

Weapons: 2 laser cannons; 2 proton torpedo launchers; 2 light ion cannons

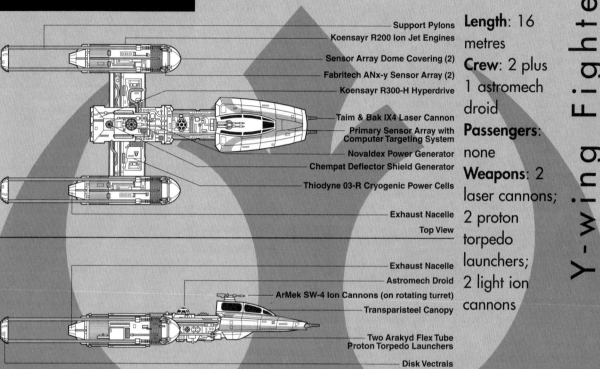

Support Pylons

Koensayr R200 Ion Jet Engines

Sensor Array Dome Covering (2)

Fabritech ANx-y Sensor Array (2)

Koensayr R300-H Hyperdrive

Taim & Bak IX4 Laser Cannon

Primary Sensor Array with Computer Targeting System

Novaldex Power Generator

Chempat Deflector Shield Generator

Thiodyne 03-R Cryogenic Power Cells

Exhaust Nacelle

Top View

Exhaust Nacelle

Astromech Droid

ArMek SW-4 Ion Cannons (on rotating turret)

Transparisteel Canopy

Two Arakyd Flex Tube Proton Torpedo Launchers

Disk Vectrals

Side View

Length: 7.4 metres
Crew: 1
Passengers: 1
Weapons: none

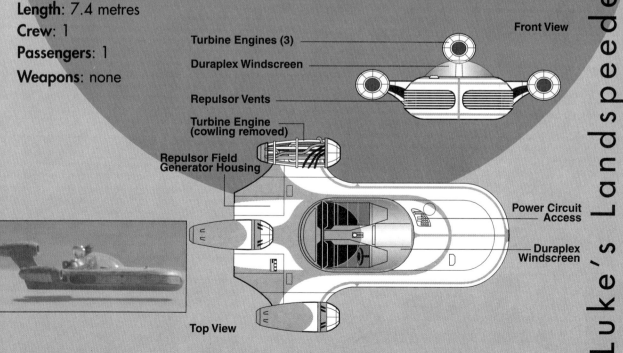

Front View

Turbine Engines (3)

Duraplex Windscreen

Repulsor Vents

Turbine Engine (cowling removed)

Repulsor Field Generator Housing

Power Circuit Access

Duraplex Windscreen

Top View

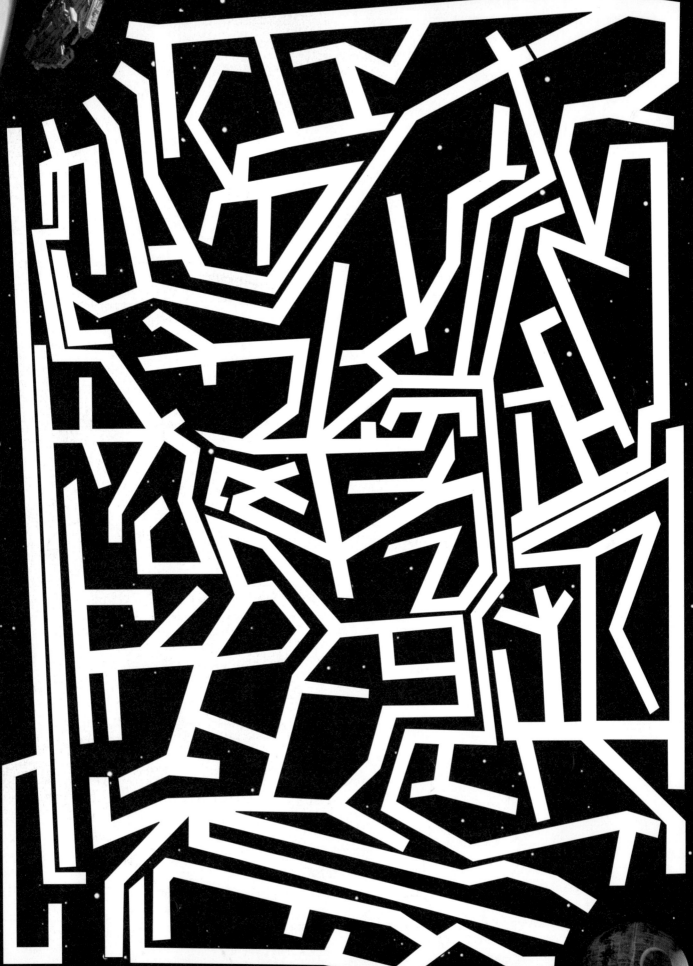

Illustrated By Simon Connor   Solution on page 61

STAR WARS™

SKYWALKERS

Join the junior section of the Official UK *Star Wars* Club

A Robell Club

If you're a Star Wars fan aged 14 or under join Skywalkers. Activate your membership with the special holograms you'll receive, and you'll be ready to join Luke Skywalker, Princess Leia, C-3PO, R2-D2 and the rest of the Rebel Alliance in a fight to the death against the evil Empire.

In your Skywalkers Pack you'll find: ✹ a letter from the Rebel Alliance with a *Star Wars* hologram ✹ a secret membership card with a different *Star Wars* hologram ✹ six exclusive collectors' cards with histories of the main characters ✹ two magnificent A3 posters ✹ a stylish Skywalkers badge ✹ an exclusive Club edition of "A Wind To Shake The Stars", first part of the original *Star Wars* radio adaptation on cassette featuring the original actors ✹ superb miniature scale models of Han Solo's *Millennium Falcon* and Darth Vader's TIE fighter ✹

And on your birthday and again at Christmas you'll get a superb card.

LF1

The Skywalkers Pack alone could cost around £17.00. But annual membership is just £12.99 including postage with a 14 day money-back guarantee if you're not delighted. To enrol: return the coupon (to be completed by an adult) to Skywalkers, P.O. Box 142, Horsham RH13 5FJ; call 01403 257755 (credit cards only); or fax 01403 261555.

te: images not to scale

PLUS FREE!

Money-saving vouchers for ily attractions all over the Save the cost of your mbership many times over! ✹

Star Wars stickers (first 000 members only). ✹

For details of the main club call 01403 257755

Please enrol the following as a member of Skywalkers at £12.99.
Member's Name: _____ Address: _____
Post Code: _____
Member's Date of birth: __/__/__ Parent/Guardian Name: _____
Your Name (if different): _____ Address: _____
Post Code: _____
☐ I enclose a cheque/ PO for the total of £_____ payable to **Star Wars** Club.
☐ Please charge the sum of £_____ to my Access/Visa
card number: ☐☐☐☐ ☐☐☐☐ ☐☐☐☐ ☐☐☐☐ Expires: ___/___
Please tick this box if you do NOT wish to receive details of similar offers from us or companies we approve ☐
WI

se note: We reserve the right to change the terms of this offer (including the contents of the Pack) at any time. After 30/6/98 please call to check that the price is still Allow 28 days for delivery. Promoter: Robell Media Promotions Limited, registered in England number 2852153. TM & © 1997 Lucasfilm Ltd. All Rights Reserved. Used Under Authorisation

STAR WARS
THE EMPIRE STRIKES BACK

It is a dark time for the Rebellion. Although the Death Star has been destroyed, Imperial troops have driven the Rebel forces from their hidden base and pursued them across the galaxy.
Evading the dreadful Imperial Starfleet, a group of freedom fighters led by Luke Skywalker

has established a new secret base on the remote ice world of Hoth. The evil lord Darth Vader, obsessed with finding young Skywalker, has dispatched thousands of remote probes into the far reaches of space...

Luke was patrolling on his tauntaun in the snowy wastes of Hoth. As he was investigating the landing of an Imperial probe, a fierce wampa snow creature attacked him. When

Luke came round, he was hanging upside down in the creature's lair... with his lightsabre just out of reach.

Using the Force to attract it to him, Luke cut himself down. The wampa lunged, and Luke fought it off. He escaped into the snow, but now without his tauntaun, he soon fell to the ground, exhausted and frozen.

Ben appeared before him. "You will go to the Dagobah system and learn from Yoda," he said.

At Echo Base, on Hoth, Han Solo had been saying goodbye to Leia, intending to resume his smuggling activities. Now, as night fell, he was searching in the snow for Luke. His tauntaun collapsed and died as Han reached Luke, now

barely alive. Han used his friend's lightsabre to cut open the tauntaun and provide a warm shelter until rescue came next day.

The landing of the probe had alerted the Rebels to an imminent attack by Darth Vader - and it wasn't long in coming. Imperial walkers, like mountain-sized metal elephants, advanced on the base, flattening everything in their path. It was a losing battle for the Rebel pilots,

and Luke was shot down by a walker. But from the ground he fired a harpoon at it, climbed the rope and blew up the walker with a landmine.

Leia supervised the evacuation of the Base, and then left with Han,

Chewie and Threepio in the *Millennium Falcon*. Luke reached base and, with Artoo, set off in his X-wing for Dagobah.

He landed there badly - in a jungle swamp. An odd little creature appeared and took him back to its ramshackle home. This was Yoda...and now Luke could begin his Jedi training!

Meanwhile, the *Falcon* had narrowly escaped destruction. But the hyperdrive wasn't working, and Han suggested they go to Cloud City for repairs. This was a thriving gas mining outpost in the sky, bustling with life and cloud cars. It was run by Han's gambling friend Lando Calrissian, who'd won the place in a game. Lando was the previous

owner of the *Falcon*, which Han had won from *him*! In Cloud City Lando greeted his visitors and gave them hospitality. But it was a trap, for bounty hunter Boba Fett and Darth Vader were waiting!

Han and Leia were treated badly. Vader wanted to lure Luke to the dark side, so that they could rule the galaxy as father and son. He knew that Luke would know, through the Force, of the danger his friends were in and come to their aid. "I love you," said Leia. "I know," replied Han, as he was cruelly carbon-frozen into a solid slab and handed over to Boba Fett.

him. They fought with lightsabres, with Vader imploring Luke to join him. Eventually Luke was trapped by Vader on a bridge over a seemingly bottomless shaft. Vader's lightsabre slashed at Luke and cut off his hand. "Your destiny lies with me, Skywalker!" he growled. Luke accused him of killing his father. "I *am* your father!" came Vader's devastating reply. Dazed and in pain, Luke fell...

On Dagobah Luke had been undergoing intensive instruction in the secrets of the Force. He sensed that Leia, Han and Chewie were in trouble and vowed to rescue them. Yoda and Ben advised against it, but Luke took off anyway.

He arrived in Cloud City and Darth Vader was ready to confront

Lando was regretting his treacherous actions. "I'm sorry. I had no choice," he tried to explain. Then he had a change of heart and fired at the troopers. With Leia, and Threepio badly

damaged and strapped to Chewie's

back, he rushed out. But Boba's ship *Slave I* - with Han on board - was already leaving.

The Rebels ran to the *Falcon*.
Thanks to Lando, its hyperdrive was

now working. As they set off, Leia
felt Luke calling, "Hear me, Leia..."
Swinging the *Falcon* round, they
found him hanging precariously on a
metal framework that had broken
his fall.

They brought him on board,

then put the *Falcon* into
hyperspace and flashed away to
rejoin the
Rebels.

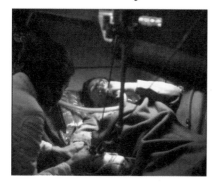

Luke was taken to the medical
ship to recover and was soon given a
new hand.

Lando and Chewbacca
prepared the *Millennium Falcon*
and set off in search of Han. They
would report back with any news
they found. Luke, Leia and the
droids watched as the *Millennium
Falcon* detached from the docking
port and blasted off into space.

STAR WARS - WEAPON TECHNOLOGY

The Lightsabre

The graceful, humming lightsabre is an ancient weapon devised by the Jedi. It commands great respect throughout the galaxy, although it is intended for use only when passive negotiation has failed. In fact, its disciplined use is learned only after many years of supervised training.

    The lightsabre's durasteel handle protects its user from the phenomenal power of its energy-blade, which can slice through almost any material - with the exception of another lightsabre blade. The handle conceals a long-lasting power source and precision-honed jewels or crystals which focus the weapon's intense light energy into a narrow, parallel beam approximately one metre in length. It is interesting to note that the energy reserve is depleted only when a lightsabre's blade touches an object. Lightsabres vary in design detail, as traditionally each one is custom-built by its possessor.

Blasters

The term 'blaster' covers weapons ranging from hand-held pistols to the huge laser cannons mounted on starships. Blaster pistols are used widely by both the Imperial forces and the Rebels. There are various types, but essentially they operate on the same principle - shooting bolts of high-power light energy through their lens system.

    Upon firing, a blaster gives off the characteristic odour of ozone. On most models the discharge power can be adjusted from 'stun' setting right up to a lethal, vaporising output.

Carbon Freezing

Though not strictly a weapon, carbon-freezing is used to very sinister effect by Darth Vader in Cloud City.

    It is actually a commercial process for storing valuable Tibanna gas in carbonite during transit. The gas is mixed with molten carbonite and instantly cooled into solid form. It can then be kept in this convenient state until release at its destination. Vader sees the potential of carbon-freezing as a secure and foolproof means of transporting Luke, upon capture, back to his master, Palpatine. Unfortunately for Han, a guinea-pig is needed to first test the safety of freezing a human. So he is forced into the chamber and turned into a ghastly living sculpture set in a giant slab of carbonite.

He is then handed over, in suspended animation, to bounty-hunter Boba Fett, who takes him back to Jabba's palace, where Han becomes a novelty wall-decoration for the amusement of the slimy gangster and his pals.

Bowcaster

A bowcaster, as carried by Chewie, is a curious Wookiee mix of advanced technology and antiquity. Essentially it is an energy-firing laser weapon, but in the easily recognised form of the traditional crossbow.

Gaffi Stick

Not all weapons in the galaxy are sophisticated, of course. After all, the Ewoks defeat the Imperial forces on Endor with little more than stones, logs and positively prehistoric hang-gliders!

The gruesome-looking gaffi stick, or gaderffii, is a prime example of the primitive technology of Tatooine's Tusken Raiders. It is the weapon favoured by this aggressive bunch and resembles a crudely formed axe. Perhaps the most pleasant thing you could say about it is that it is a 'green' product - made from scrap metal removed from wrecked craft abandoned on Tatooine!

REBEL PROFILE

Name: Lando Calrissian
Genus: Human
Hair: Black
Eyes: Brown
Height: 1.78 metres
Home: Unknown

Lando is the shady galactic gambler with a dash of style and a disarming smile!

Leia has her doubts about this charmer's integrity right from the start, when Han flies into Cloud City to call on his friendly rival of old. Lando greets the Princess gallantly with a kiss to the hand, despite the fact that he's played his double-dealing part in a conspiracy with Vader to trap her and Han.

Lando is a successful opportunist who's doing well out of the gas mining city he owns, and he doesn't want to rock the boat. "I have just made a deal that will keep the Empire out of here for ever," he admits, leading Han and Leia straight into Vader's arms.

But underneath he has a noble heart. He soon turns his back on smuggling to devote his considerable life-skills to the cause of freedom - winding up as a Rebel general and hero in *Return of the Jedi*!

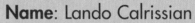

Lando at the controls of the *Millennium Falcon*

Lando greeting Leia at Cloud City

LANDO CALRISSIAN

REBEL PROFILE

Name: Yoda
Genus: Not known
Hair: White
Eyes: Brown
Height: 0.66 metres
Home: Dagobah

Yoda may be wizened and rather eccentric in his ways - and at 900 years old, he's perfectly entitled to be! But this curious little fellow is merely putting on an act by chuckling and appearing bumbling when he finds Luke and R2-D2 crash-landed in the swamp on Dagobah. Only when he's checked out Luke's motives for coming, do we hear the learned tones of the real Yoda, Jedi Master. His endearing speech pattern remains, however, as when he says, "Away put your weapon!"

He's hardly what you'd expect a Jedi Master to look like but he explains to Luke that it's a mistake to judge by size. "Try, not. Do - or do not," he urges, using the Force alone to lift the massive weight of Luke's ship effortlessly from the swamp.

He's ailing in *Return of the Jedi* but fades away in the knowledge that Luke, once he has faced Vader, will truly be a Jedi Knight.

R2-D2 attempts to get back the torch

Yoda's hut in the swamp

YODA

EMPIRE PROFILE

Name: Emperor Palpatine
Genus: Human
Hair: Grey-brown
Eyes: Orange
Height: 1.73 metres
Home: Not known

If anyone is ripe for a makeover, it's the Emperor! With only a chilling death-mask of a face peeping from his sinister hooded cloak, he's more like the Grim Reaper than master of the galaxy.

For thousands of years the Old Republic had brought harmony to the galaxy, but it became poisoned with corruption. Seen as a promising leader who would restore credibility to the government, Senator Palpatine was made President. But he proceeded to abuse his new position by creating the New Order and declaring himself Emperor.

Now ruling with a network of immense military might, he uses the Force to his advantage and recognises all too clearly the threat that Luke poses to his Empire. He's convinced that the young Jedi Knight can be drawn to the dark side but, as we see, that is his biggest mistake - and his downfall. For, in his final confrontation with Luke, Vader turns on his master and hurls him to his doom...

EMPEROR PALPATINE

EMPIRE PROFILE

Name: Boba Fett
Genus: Human
Hair: Not known
Eyes: Not known
Height: 1.83 metres
Home: Not known

Here's someone you wouldn't want to meet on a dark night...or any night, come to that. Boba Fett is a bounty hunter, notorious throughout the galaxy. His formidable armour is derived from that of the evil Mandalorians, who fought in the earlier Clone Wars. Boba's built-in weaponry includes lasers on his wrists, a magnetic grappling hook and a deadly flame projector. It's his jet backpack that proves his undoing in *Return of the Jedi*: it is hit by Han's lance and propels him helplessly into the lair of the dreaded Sarlacc!

Name: IG-88
Genus: Droid
Hair: None
Eye sensors: Red
Height: 1.96 metres
Home: Halowan Laboratories

There's certainly no mistaking this cool customer or his purpose in life. The nightmarish IG-88 makes even Boba Fett look friendly!

He's an assassin droid who has developed a one-track mind of his own and is making his way in the galaxy. He operates as a bounty hunter, one of the number hired by Darth Vader after the Battle of Hoth to locate the *Millennium Falcon* and apprehend the Rebels.

BOBA FETT / IG-88

Hoth

Brrr! If ever there was an unlikely place for the Rebel Alliance to build their Echo Base, it has to be the ice world of Hoth. And that's precisely why they chose it.

This bleak, white planet in the remote star system of Hoth has little to offer in the way of comfort. By day the heavily-clad Rebels can just about bear the freezing cold as they go about their duties. However, at night the temperature drops to such unbearable levels that it's vital for everyone to remain inside the Base with the huge, insulating doors firmly closed.

The hardy tauntauns with their thick fur prove useful for personal transport and as beasts of burden. But also native to Hoth are the wampas - vicious and powerful snow creatures who live in ice caves. They hunt for prey and store their victims live, as Luke discovers almost to his cost in *The Empire Strikes Back*.

The landing of the Imperial probe on Hoth is a terrible blow to the Rebels. It sends out a signal indicating life on the planet, which the intuitive Vader interprets correctly as meaning he's found the Rebels. In the terrible battle that follows on Hoth, many Rebels perish in their valiant fight to save Echo Base.

Dagobah

There are few inhabitants in the Dagobah star system, and the swampy jungle planet of Dagobah is the adopted home of the solitary Yoda. He lives there in self-imposed isolation in order to avoid being a target for elimination in the Empire's relentless drive against the Jedi Knights.

Dagobah is a lonely place, to say the least. Covered in mist, it discourages inquisitive travellers, and even Luke crash-lands in the swamp when he comes in search of Yoda.

It remains an undeveloped planet, rich in the vegetation which provides all the food Yoda needs to remain self-sufficient in his tiny hut made from natural materials. When Luke first arrives, the hospitable Yoda takes him back home for some rootleaf stew!

Secluded Dagobah provides a good training ground for Luke to run and jump and learn his new skills. Yoda puts him through an intensive programme of physical and psychological exercises. It's also the scene of Luke's important lesson about the dangers of the dark side: he has a surreal encounter with a vision of Vader, in which he unmasks the Dark Lord - only to find that it is *himself*!

43

AT-AT Walker

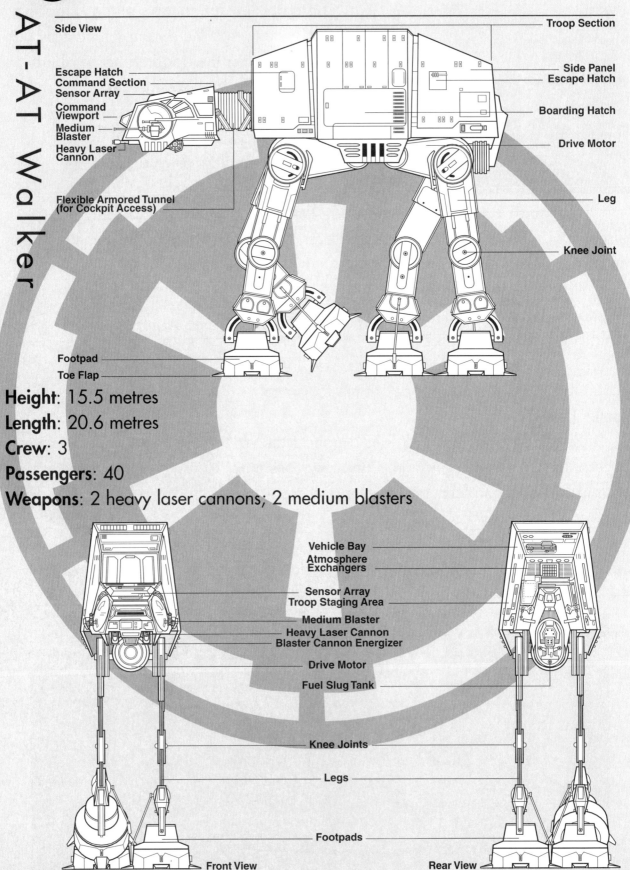

Side View

Escape Hatch
Command Section
Sensor Array
Command Viewport
Medium Blaster
Heavy Laser Cannon

Flexible Armored Tunnel (for Cockpit Access)

Footpad
Toe Flap

Troop Section
Side Panel
Escape Hatch
Boarding Hatch
Drive Motor
Leg
Knee Joint

Height: 15.5 metres

Length: 20.6 metres

Crew: 3

Passengers: 40

Weapons: 2 heavy laser cannons; 2 medium blasters

Vehicle Bay
Atmosphere Exchangers
Sensor Array
Troop Staging Area
Medium Blaster
Heavy Laser Cannon
Blaster Cannon Energizer
Drive Motor
Fuel Slug Tank

Knee Joints

Legs

Footpads

Front View

Rear View

EMPIRE PROFILE

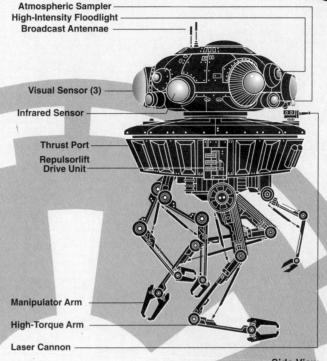

Atmospheric Sampler
High-Intensity Floodlight
Broadcast Antennae

Visual Sensor (3)

Infrared Sensor

Thrust Port

Repulsorlift
Drive Unit

Manipulator Arm

High-Torque Arm

Laser Cannon

Side View

Length: 21.5 metres

Crew: 1

Passengers: 6 prisoners

Weapons: 2 twin-mounted blaster cannons; concussion missile tube launcher; ion cannon; tractor beam projector; 2 proton torpedo launchers

Front View

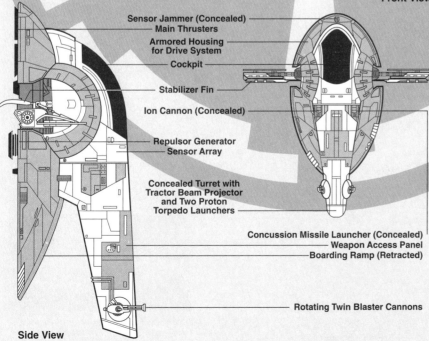

Sensor Jammer (Concealed)
Main Thrusters

Armored Housing
for Drive System

Cockpit

Stabilizer Fin

Ion Cannon (Concealed)

Repulsor Generator
Sensor Array

Concealed Turret with
Tractor Beam Projector
and Two Proton
Torpedo Launchers

Concussion Missile Launcher (Concealed)
Weapon Access Panel
Boarding Ramp (Retracted)

Rotating Twin Blaster Cannons

Side View

Slave I

Snowspeeder

Length: 5.3 metres
Crew: 2
Passengers: None
Weapons: Double laser cannon; power harpoon

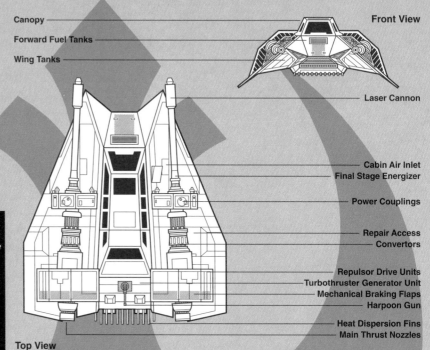

Canopy
Forward Fuel Tanks
Wing Tanks

Front View

Laser Cannon

Cabin Air Inlet
Final Stage Energizer

Power Couplings

Repair Access
Convertors

Repulsor Drive Units
Turbothruster Generator Unit
Mechanical Braking Flaps
Harpoon Gun

Heat Dispersion Fins
Main Thrust Nozzles

Top View

Cloud Car

Armored Canopy

Side View

Blaster Cannon
Sensor Suite
Armor Plating

Landing Gear (retracted)
Maneuvering Flap

Length: 7 metres
Crew: 1
Passengers: 1
Weapons: Double blaster cannon

Blaster
Gunnery Officer's
Connecting
Ion/Repulsorlift
Pilot's Pod

Blaster

Sensor

Landing Gear

Front View

DEATH STAR MAZE

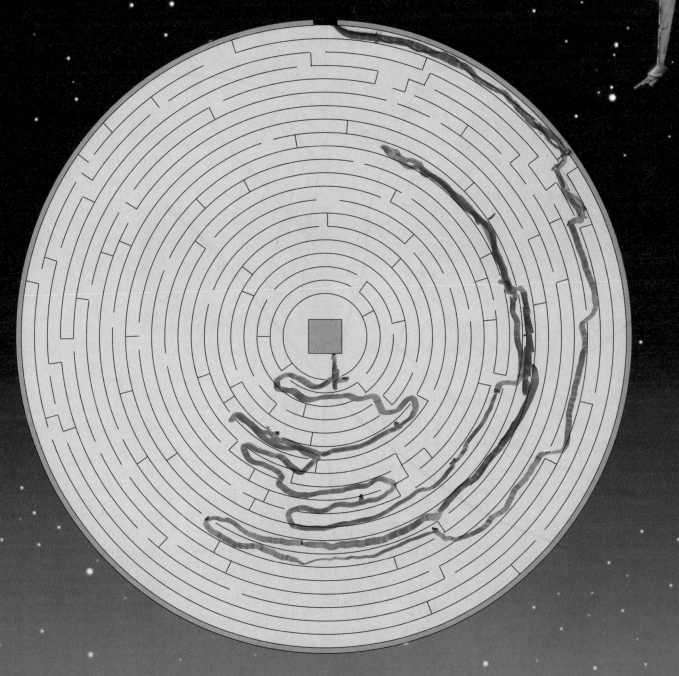

Can you guide the squadron to the reactor core and destroy the Death Star?

Illustrated By: Simon Connor Solution on page 61

STAR WARS
RETURN OF THE JEDI

Luke Skywalker has returned to his home planet of Tatooine in an attempt to rescue his friend Han

Solo from the clutches of the vile gangster Jabba the Hutt. Little does Luke know that the GALACTIC EMPIRE has secretly begun construction on a new armoured space station even more powerful than the first dreaded Death Star. When completed, this ultimate weapon will spell certain doom for the small band of Rebels struggling to restore freedom to the galaxy...

Artoo and Threepio arrived at the entrance to Jabba the Hutt's palace on Tatooine. They were taken to the throne room where Jabba sat with his friends. Artoo projected a big hologram of Luke, offering his two droids for Han's

freedom. But it was a waste of time: Jabba kept Threepio and Artoo anyway.

The following day a bounty

hunter brought in Chewie. He agreed to a price with Jabba. Chewie was imprisoned, and a party followed.

Later the bounty hunter slipped into the throne room, found the carbon-frozen Han hanging on the

wall and freed him. He came back to life but couldn't see at first. "Who are you?" he asked. "Someone who loves you," came the reply. The bounty hunter was Leia!

But Jabba was waiting. Leia was chained up and kept by his throne, and Han was thrown into a cell with Chewie.

Next, Luke, now in Jedi robes, came to the palace and demanded the release of Han. Jabba opened up the floor and Luke fell into a pit, the lair of the rancor beast. Luke killed it...but there was still more trouble ahead.

Jabba, with Leia on a chain, set off across the desert in his sail barge. Luke, Han and Chewie, in a skiff, were being taken to the pit

where the deadly Sarlacc creature lived. Jabba and his pals would watch them die! A guard pushed Luke off a plank over the pit. But Luke leapt backwards and used the Force to bring his lightsabre out of Artoo.

A grim battle followed, during which Leia pulled her chain round Jabba's neck and finished him off.

Along with Luke, Han, Chewie and the two droids, she escaped in the skiff as the sail barge blew up.

Yoda was very weak when Luke visited him on Dagobah "Soon will I rest...

forever sleep," he sighed.

He urged Luke to confront Darth Vader, explaining that only then would he be a true Jedi Knight. He also admitted that Vader was Luke's father. With that, Yoda closed his eyes and faded away.

Obi-Wan Kenobi's image appeared before Luke, telling him that he had trained Luke's father, Anakin, before he turned into Vader. Ben also made another startling revelation: Leia was Luke's sister!

The Rebels were ready to attack the almost complete second Death Star. The plan was to use the *Tydirium*, a stolen Imperial shuttle, to penetrate the Empire's defences

on the little moon of Endor and destroy the source of the energy shield protecting the Death Star. This would allow Rebel ships to fire on the Death Star.

Luke, Leia, Han and Chewie took off in the *Tydirium*. Luke felt he shouldn't really be with them, for he sensed that Vader knew he was coming.

They landed on Endor and found themselves in a forest, where they saw two scout troopers. Han and Chewie went to deal with them - but there were more troopers. Luke and Leia leapt onto speeder bikes and gave chase.

Eventually Luke returned to Han, Chewie and the droids, but  Leia had been stranded in the forest. A furry Ewok creature befriended her and took her back to his village. There she was reunited with Han, Luke and Chewie, who had been captured by Ewoks. In the evening they gathered round a campfire with the Ewoks, and later Luke told Leia she was his twin sister.

It was time for Luke to meet Darth Vader. He surrendered and was taken to the  Death Star. Vader brought him before Emperor Palpatine, who told Luke that a trap lay in wait for his friends at the bunker on Endor. Luke brandished his lightsabre, but Vader was ready to defend his master. Father and son fought violently.

 Luke injured Vader but spared his life.

"Fulfil your destiny and take your father's place at my side," snapped the Emperor. When Luke refused,  Palpatine used blue Force lightning from his fingers to send the young Jedi reeling to the floor. "Father... please!" cried Luke in agony.

Vader paused, then the good rose inside him and he saved his son by hurling the Emperor down a bottomless shaft. Then as Luke tended to him, Vader asked his son to remove his mask, saying, "Let me  look on you with my own eyes." Without the mask, he was unable to breathe, and he died.

Meanwhile, there had been a  trap on Endor. Troops were waiting for Leia, Han and Chewie.

But suddenly the Ewoks appeared in force. Using catapults, slings, rocks, rolling logs and even crude hang-gliders, they defeated the Imperial forces. The Rebels set charges in the bunker and demolished it. The energy shield was gone, and the waiting Rebel ships could reach the Death Star!

In the *Millennium Falcon*, Lando Calrissian - now a Rebel

general - raced towards the Death Star's reactor, followed by a squad of TIE fighters.

Lando fired his missiles at the reactor core and zoomed away as fast as the *Millennium Falcon* would go in the space.

There was a huge explosion and the massive Death Star was ripped apart...

...only seconds after Luke, bringing the body of his father with him, had made his escape in a shuttle.

Now he would return to his victorious comrades and the Ewoks waiting on Endor.

Endor and the Ewoks

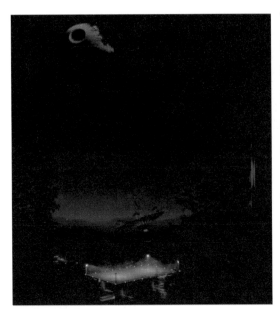

There's nothing particularly exciting or out of the ordinary about the Endor star system. Galactically speaking, it lies off the beaten track...and that's what makes it the perfect spot for the unobtrusive completion of the mighty second Death Star battle station!

The Moon of Endor is covered with tall forests and was chosen by the Empire to quietly site the energy shield generator protecting the Death Star from attack. The rough terrain doesn't present any problems for the chicken-legged scout walkers or the scout troopers on their repulsorlift speeder bikes.

There are numerous species indigenous to Endor, but the Imperial forces don't perceive any of them as a threat to their ambitious domination plans. They haven't, of course, bargained on the wily Ewoks!

Luke, Han and Chewie may have a size advantage and advanced laser weapon technology - but it doesn't stop them from being trapped in a net by the primitive little Ewoks and taken prisoner!

These shy, furry creatures, standing around a metre high, live in villages high in the trees of Endor. Despite being prehistoric in their ways - and still using bows and arrows for hunting - they are clever and brave. Without their enthusiastic help in *Return of the Jedi*, the Rebels would have failed to sabotage the energy shield...and the future of the galaxy would be very different indeed.

It's the inquisitive Wicket. W Warrick who finds Leia lost in the forest, and he's the one who urges his tribe to help the Rebels with their mission. And if you think Ewoks are cute, just take a look at their babies!

Teebo

Chief Chirpa

Ewok

Ewok

Wicket

Jabba's Throne Room

To describe Jabba's guards as pig-like is really rather an insult to pigs! Once you get past these surly beasts and into the throne room of the gigantic desert

palace, that's when the fun starts...if you can call it fun, that is.

Crime lord Jabba spends his leisure hours enjoying the more decadent pleasures of life, surrounded by dancers, droids, wretched servants and a guest-list of alien and humanoid criminal types. The secret of enjoying yourself is to keep on the right side of the intolerant Jabba -

or else. That's a lesson the court jester, little monkey-lizard Salacious Crumb, learned very quickly.

But at least the music's good when Jabba's partying. It's provided by the tuneful talents of Max Rebo, Droopy McCool and singers Sy Snootles and Joh Yowzah.

REBEL PROFILE

Name: Mon Mothma
Genus: Human
Hair: Auburn
Eyes: Green-blue
Height: 1.5 metres
Home: Chandrila

Leader of the Rebels is Mon Mothma, a resolute woman of the highest principles, who is totally dedicated to restoring freedom to the galaxy.

As a Senator, she saw at first-hand the corruption growing in the Old Republic and the rise to power of Emperor Palpatine. Initially she struggled against the evil from within the Senate. But, recognising that she was fighting a losing battle, she was forced to go underground and form a resistance movment. The Rebel Alliance was born!

Name: Admiral Ackbar
Genus: Mon Calamari
Hair: None
Eyes: Orange
Height: 1.88 metres
Home: Mon Calamari

The amphibious admiral is one of Mon Mothma's two senior military advisors. A skilled tactician, he's the brains behind the successful strategy to destroy the second Death Star and end the terrible new threat it poses to the galaxy.

Ackbar comes from the watery planet of Mon Calamari, whose inhabitants are fervent supporters of the Rebel cause. These intelligent, peace-loving people were cruelly treated by the Empire, who regarded non-human species as inferior and invaded Mon Calamari to enslave its population.

MON MOTHMA / ADMIRAL ACKBAR

GALAXY PROFILE

The Rancor

Jabba has a novel floorshow to provide amusement for his pals and himself. He feeds his enemies - and anyone else he tires of - to the bloodthirsty rancor! This huge monster with fangs and sharp claws lives below his throne room. When Oola the dancer pulls away from Jabba on her chain, he simply opens up the floor beneath her...

Luke arrives at Jabba's court - and he almost suffers the same fate. He has no choice but to kill the rancor by throwing a skull at a control panel and bringing down a huge steel door on the beast. At this, the rancor's trainer bursts into tears!

The Sarlacc

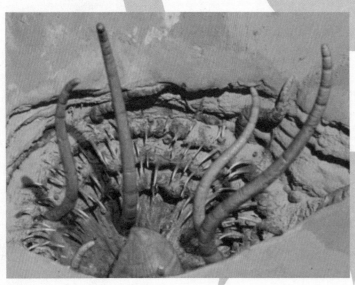

When the rancor comes to a sticky end, Jabba has another nasty trick up his sleeve for Luke and Han. He takes them, along with his entourage, to the Great Pit of Carkoon in the Dune Sea...lair of the Sarlacc.

This is a terrifying creature which lies in the pit and uses its long tentacles to grab passing victims and then pull them down into its cavernous mouth filled with sharp teeth. A slow and painful death awaits its prey: the Sarlacc doesn't hurry its meals - taking a thousand years to digest its food!

RANCOR / SARLACC PIT

EMPIRE PROFILE

Name: Scout Trooper & Snowtrooper
Genus: Human
Hair: Not known
Eyes: Not known
Height: 1.83 metres average
Home: Not known

Not only does the Emperor command a seemingly endless supply of Imperial stormtroopers to enforce his iron will, but he has specialised units too. Snowtroopers wear armour equipped with extra internal heating, so they can operate in harsh, icy environments such as we find on Hoth.

But scout troopers, seen in action on the Moon of Endor, are built for speed! They have lighter armour to give them vital extra mobility when patrolling on their speeder bikes.

Name: Royal Guard
Genus: Human
Hair: Not known
Eyes: Not known
Height: 1.83 metres average
Home: Not known

The imposing scarlet red robes and helmets of the mysterious Imperial Royal Guards somehow make them even more frightening than the stormtrooper ranks from which they are hand-picked! These elite, armoured bodyguards are deadly in combat and their traditional weapon is the force pike they carry on view. Selected for their loyalty, superior strength and intelligence, they report directly to the Emperor. Royal Guards remain constantly by his side, accompanying him on his travels by shuttle too.

TROOPERS / ROYAL GUARD

GALAXY PROFILE

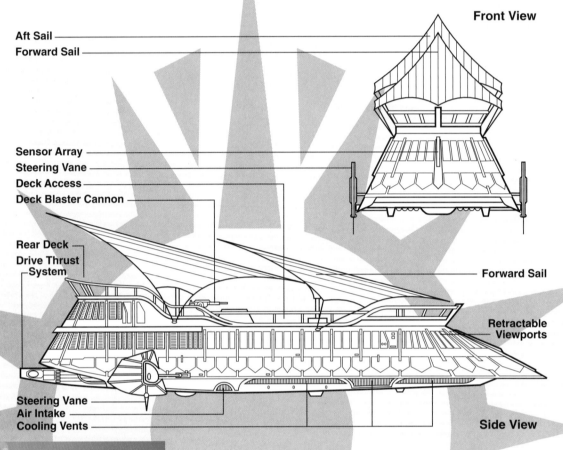

Front View

Aft Sail

Forward Sail

Sensor Array

Steering Vane

Deck Access

Deck Blaster Cannon

Rear Deck

Drive Thrust System

Forward Sail

Retractable Viewports

Steering Vane

Air Intake

Cooling Vents

Side View

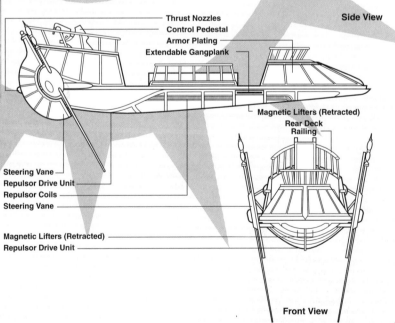

Thrust Nozzles

Control Pedestal

Armor Plating

Extendable Gangplank

Side View

Magnetic Lifters (Retracted)

Rear Deck Railing

Steering Vane

Repulsor Drive Unit

Repulsor Coils

Steering Vane

Magnetic Lifters (Retracted)

Repulsor Drive Unit

Front View

EMPIRE PROFILE

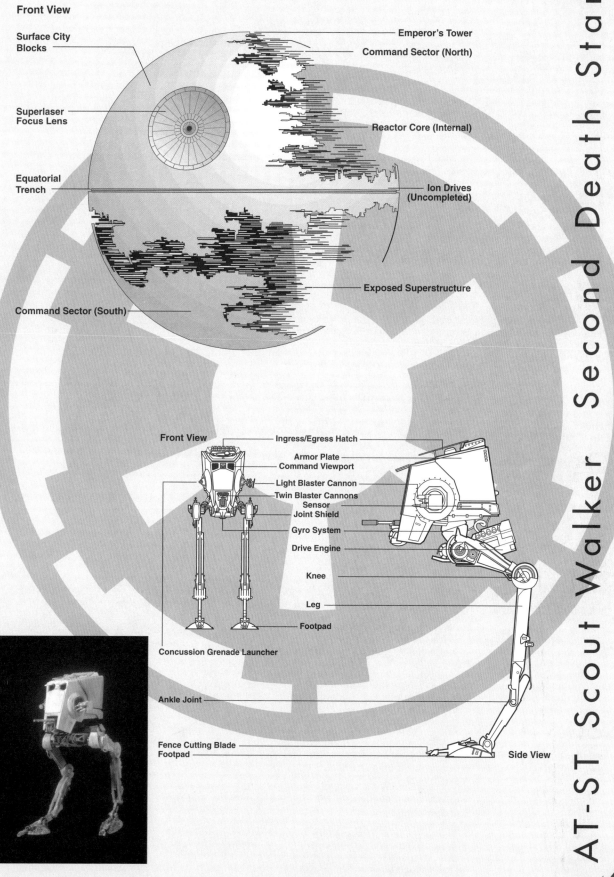

Front View

Surface City
Blocks

Superlaser
Focus Lens

Equatorial
Trench

Command Sector (South)

Emperor's Tower

Command Sector (North)

Reactor Core (Internal)

Ion Drives
(Uncompleted)

Exposed Superstructure

Front View

Ingress/Egress Hatch

Armor Plate
Command Viewport

Light Blaster Cannon

Twin Blaster Cannons
Sensor
Joint Shield

Gyro System

Drive Engine

Knee

Leg

Footpad

Concussion Grenade Launcher

Ankle Joint

Fence Cutting Blade
Footpad

Side View

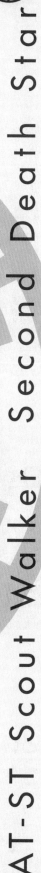

AT-ST Scout Walker Second Death Star

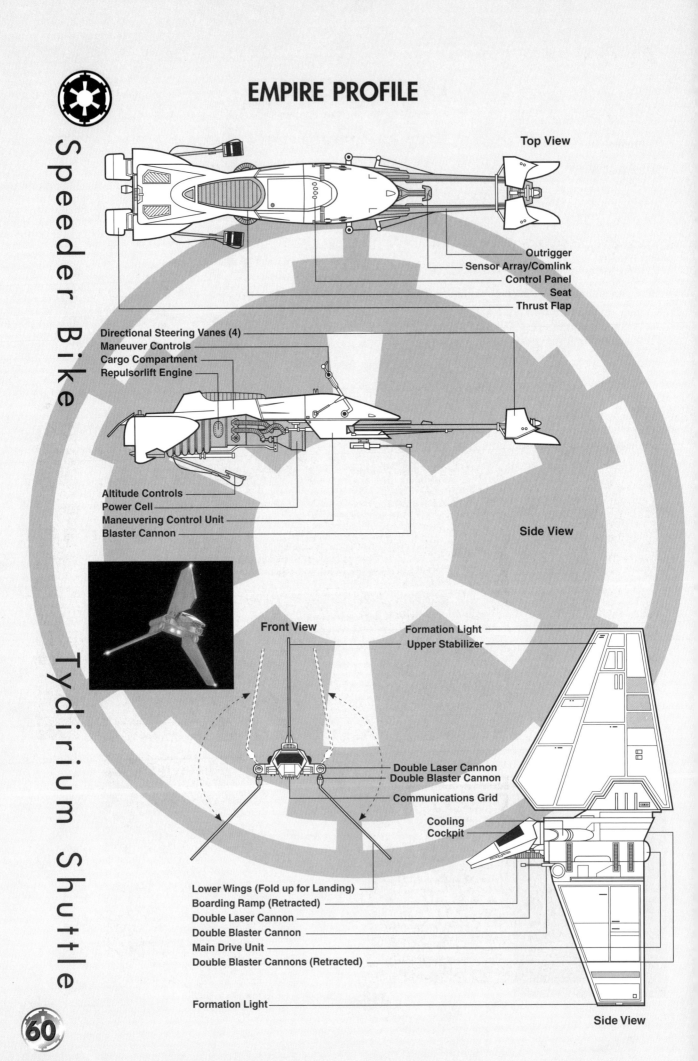

EMPIRE PROFILE

Speeder Bike

Tydirium Shuttle

Top View

Outrigger
Sensor Array/Comlink
Control Panel
Seat
Thrust Flap

Directional Steering Vanes (4)
Maneuver Controls
Cargo Compartment
Repulsorlift Engine

Altitude Controls
Power Cell
Maneuvering Control Unit
Blaster Cannon

Side View

Front View

Formation Light
Upper Stabilizer

Double Laser Cannon
Double Blaster Cannon

Communications Grid

Cooling
Cockpit

Lower Wings (Fold up for Landing)
Boarding Ramp (Retracted)
Double Laser Cannon
Double Blaster Cannon
Main Drive Unit
Double Blaster Cannons (Retracted)

Formation Light

Side View

And next...?

The menacing Death Star is no more - blown into millions of scattered pieces. The blinding flash of its destruction momentarily lights up the darkness of space like a beacon symbolising a new beginning for the galaxy.

Princess Leia, Luke, Han, Chewie and the two droids join the Ewoks in a big party to celebrate their monumental victory. The evil Palpatine is gone. Luke has been united with the twin sister he never knew. And Leia and Han have declared their love for one another.

Luke smiles as he sees that his father - now Anakin Skywalker once more - has taken his place beside Yoda and Ben. The young Jedi Knight fervently hopes that oppression and cruelty have now given way to peace and harmony in the galaxy. But who knows? Only time will tell...

MAZE SOLUTIONS

From page 30

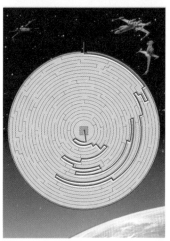

From page 47